LIVING WITH A MADMAN IN TOW

Poems of the dark and light sides of life

Keith Pierre Power

authorHOUSE®

AuthorHouse™
1663 Liberty Drive
Bloomington, IN 47403
www.authorhouse.com
Phone: 1-800-839-8640

First published by AuthorHouse 10/12/2009

ISBN: 978-1-4490-3155-8 (e)
ISBN: 978-1-4490-3153-4 (sc)
ISBN: 978-1-4490-3154-1 (hc)

Manuscript editing by: Barbara Bell Shiny Object Creative
Barbara@ShinyObjectCreative.com
www.shinnyobjectcreative.com

Cover and photo work by:
Pam Kaltenrieder
Pamstreat@gmail.com

Printed in the United States of America
Bloomington, Indiana

This book is printed on acid-free paper.

Dedication

I dedicate the book, first and foremost, to TT. Her love in our togetherness, her acceptance along the way, and her standing up to me in the end, helped make me be a better, kinder, gentler person. Without her and the good and bad memories we shared I would not have become the great man I am today. I am truly indebted to her. I thank her with all my heart. I think of TT every day as she remains my inspiration with her sweet gentle and true ways. To this day I love and miss her very much.

Secondly, to my Mom for just being Mom. And for helping me with some misadventures along the way. I love you very much.

Lastly to all the people, knowing and unknowing that guided me in this magical thing called life. Thank you.

Contents

Introduction

Abraham Lincoln wrote:

"I am not bound to win, but I am bound to be true.
I am not bound to succeed, but I am bound to live up to the light I have"

The main reason this book of poetry came about was my self assessment of who I am and who I became. This was done through Integrated Life Coaching and the Life Blueprinting process that was developed by Debbie Ford (www.debbieford.com). It is an examination of the dark and light sides of my life. I am not much different than a lot of other people who have been lost in their own self victimization, the blaming of others, and life situations for the way they are now. These things only prevent us from becoming who we are meant to be.

We can let the dark side rule our lives, or learn from it and increase the light that sets us free. This book was my process and is not intended to be answers for anyone else. However, it may raise questions and may help you on your journey through life.

Each and every one of us has a madman in tow. It is how we deal with him/her that directly affects our outcomes in life. It is about being a victim of yourself and becoming a victor over your own self loathing.

There are vision statements with my free thoughts throughout the book.

Please read the book with a grain of salt, take from it if it is of benefit to you, and disregard it if it isn't. Either way, seek out your light and keep at bay the madman in tow.

Vision Statement

"I will live in my integrity with dedication and commitment to myself, the ones I love, the ones that will teach me, and the ones that will learn from or through me.

"God will give me what I need not what I want Hopefully, some day my need and want will be the same."

A Child of Vision

A child of vision has such a decision
A decision of life
And of death
A child of vision sees everything
But can't say it did
A child of vision is of the universe
Seeing everything
Knowing right from wrong
But cannot act on either
A child of vision is incorruptible
And is accepting of all
Knowing tranquility and interconnectedness
Until you influence it
A child of vision has such a decision
A decision of life
And of death
A child of vision sees everything
But can not say it did
You see, the child of vision
Is in your mind

A House Is Not a Home

A house is not a home
Without someone to love in it
It is only a shack not worth fixing
A place to keep pending weather off
Without the love of another to share it with
The house is an empty vessel
Just like our heart's longing for the fulfillment of itself
Our hearts can be full with our self love
But remain empty until the heart of another fills it beyond capacity
You can adorn a house with wonderful things
But it remains longing in its ugliness
Without a heart's desire to share it with
A house is not a home
Without someone loving in it
A home can be but a shack
Full of love and joy
Because a home is a place full of love and laughter
But a house full of misery and unneeded things
Will only bring you but love's longing for itself
A house is not a home without love
I'll take a home full of love
Over a house full of envy any day
I want nothing more than the love of another
To make my house a home

"Being negative
Is not helping you in being positive
So, what are you going to do?"

2

A Signpost of your Becoming

Please but never be
But yourself with me
For all you see is me unsheathed
I may be but a signpost on your journey through life
Teaching you tidbits of yourself to yourself
So you can have the best of yourself to offer another
I am not always wise
But neither am I stupid
But, I can see
When you play the role of chameleon
Chameleoning on a whim
To forget about
Whatever else is going on
Avoiding the pain of past sins
I am not the one
That caused that pain
But, my tidbits of knowledge and love
Can and will cause reflection
Onto that pain and yourself
This knowledge will help you love yourself and another
When I see the true unsheathed you,
 I see only the blue sky shimmering upon a lake
Moving to the rippling water
All natural, still, pure, and beautiful
When you are with me
Be free to be you
And run naked
Though the woods of our togetherness
And know that you are safe and free with me
It is the true you
That you and I seek
To spend time with
For within that friendship

The wisdom and knowledge
I have to offer you
Will become part of your wisdom and knowledge
That will allow you
To love yourself and another
These tidbits of knowledge that are good for you
Are the same things
That bind me
And are the cross I bear
For when I share these things
All we become is friends
As you grow and heal
You will find a love
That you can and will
Only be but yourself with
And with the coming of new love for you
Our friendship will fade
To a whispering shadow
Upon your heart
And a signpost of your becoming

Alternative ending add on

I will be saddened
Yet grateful of your becoming
Because in the end
I wish it had been me
That you love

About Sex

Speak to us about sex Master
What can I say about it?
Other than it is a carnal act
It is not the making of love
But rather like two dogs fucking
That any animal can do
Even the ones that are considered retarded can
It is a primal instinct
Designed for procreation
For the continuance of a species
Nothing more, nothing less
Yes, there is gratification of release in man
A status symbol and an ego trip with no real meaning
But to gloat, it felt good at the time
Mindlessly thinking it is the right thing to do for the times
To me it still remains only two dogs fucking
No respect
No dignity
No commitment
No meaning
And no emotion
But, if you want to talk about love
The building and making of love
And how it makes one feel and act
I can speak for hours
As for me speaking further on sex
There is nothing further to say
The release is done
Short, not so sweet and to no purpose
Just like unmeaning sex itself
Next

Acceptance

They say accept the things you can not change
And learn not just through your own understanding
But all man's knowledge and understanding
How do you accept the things you cannot change?
It is the challenge of your own understanding of yourself
In order to accept the changing challenges of life
For they are not set out by you
But rather Creator itself
You are Creator's toy or muse?
As he plays with your own understanding of yourself
So you can learn acceptance of the way things are
And not to hope for the things you cannot have or change
Acceptance holds happiness and appreciation
Acceptance holds sadness and despair
No matter what the situation is
It is how you deal with it
Whether or not you accept what's happening
These challenges of acceptance can be like a battle
A battle between happiness and sadness and good and evil
How are you going to let your ego play on you?
What are you going to do?
Are you going to be happy for the change and or the challenge?
Or are you going to let it eat at you and zap your energy?
Non-acceptance will eat you away
But acceptance will set you free
Why are you letting yourself be bound to any situation negatively?
Accept the things you can not change
And move on
Move on to new challenges
Free from past non-accepting resistance
And learn from all man's knowledge and understanding of acceptance

Not just your wounded egos knowledge of non - acceptance
These challenges set out before you are just that - challenges
Put there by your Creator to test you
To see if you're strong enough to accept
And push on through life's journey
To become a stronger person
A person that accepts and adapts
Adapts to the challenges of life set out before him
Without acceptance to changes in our life
We will be forever weak
Too weak to go forth and live
Live a stronger better life
A life with greater joy and challenges with gratitude and acceptance
You will have peace with yourself
When acceptance is granted by you
Change is inevitable
In doing so accept them willingly
In that you will have the strength to change what you can
And the knowledge to see and act on the difference
Acceptance to all things is what new beginnings are made of
So accept life graciously

"People do not live by knowledge alone but by the love that comes from those who have crossed our paths"

Are You Afraid It Might Be Real?

Are you afraid it might be real?
What I have to offer
I have but only three things I can offer you
I have myself to give
My love to share
And my commitment onto you
With nothing to hide
And it is true and real
These things I have to offer you
I do not think they will keep you from just being
Being who you are
With me
Or with the world you choose to live with
Are you afraid it might be real?
That I just want you, the you, you are
Unyielding to anyone but yourself
Or are you afraid it might be real?
And you don't know how to deal with it
Because you've never had it and it's new to you
Is that what makes you afraid?
And why would you push it away?
Is the change too big for you?
Are you afraid you're not good enough?
To have something real
Or is it that there is no challenge to change me
Because I am already what you've longed for
And there is no work involved to get it
Is it freaking you out?
Now that it stands before you
Willing to offer you more
Than you ever had before

With anyone else
Are you still afraid it might be real?
And you don't quite know what or how to feel
What do you have to lose?
Is it the freedom of being alone?
The safety in aloneness?
Your independence?
Your anger or hatred?
The lust of the choosing?
Or the muse of the chasing?
If this is the case there's nothing real to lose
And everything superficial to gain
At the expense of the other
But this is not what you say you want
You say you want the love of another
And that you're not afraid of the real thing
What of your actions?
They speak a different way
They say you are afraid of the real thing
Then what is it that you seek?
Is the man that is chasing not of your liking?
Do I have too little to offer?
Because I have no material wealth
If this is what you seek
I must bow my head and withdraw
For my wealth comes from my heart
That could adorn you for a lifetime
With much more value
Then what material wealth will ever have
Or is it that I'm just not of your liking?
Is there no oh lala?
Or are you afraid it might be real?
And you don't know how to deal with the feelings
Or you don't want to deal with them
So please tell me
Why are you afraid it might be real?

Break the Chains That Bind You

How will I break the chains that bind me?
How will I seek this freedom?
Let alone achieve
Are my hands bound by my past events?
Frankly, am I bound by past failings?
Longing for more
How will the binding chains on me be unlocked?
Is it I must acknowledge my fears and failures
Or is it just the ability to accept them
Knowing that they are there
Knowing that they can make me uncomfortable
Knowing they can make me make mistakes
Mistakes in my judgement and decisions
Keeping me from achieving more of what I want
Will people love me if I show these flaws?
Will I love myself?
If I slow and use them
Or will I remain a victim of my own self-loathing
Hating the parts of me that were shunned
But using them as a scapegoat to get out of something
Or using them to get something I haven't earned
Love isn't bound by these chains
But have I tried to bind love to them
Frankly, what am I fearing?
Is it myself?
Or is it what others will see, then expect
Is it success?
Or is it failure?
Or maybe it's both
Could it be what I may have not ever had, needed or wanted
I don't know

But frankly I must break these chains that bind me
For these chains are my failing
How will I get along without these chains?
I have never lived without them
Since I let myself and others create them
How will I explain myself?
Since these chains have become my excuses
The chains have become too easy for me
To manipulate my false needs with
I cannot ask for help in removing these chains
I must do it myself
But can I deal with showing me
Me without the chains that bind me
They have been my fiercest foe
And my dearest friend
Yet I know the chains have prevented me from achieving my whole
I guess it's time to break the chains
And let go of past fear and failings
To face the future as a beginning of a new day
And remind myself each day
That the chains are just a negative thought away
And when I deny myself and the world around me
The greatness of me
I am only reinforcing the chains that bound me
For far too long
Will this new acceptance of me set me free?
Free from the chains that bound me
I hope so
For it is this chainless freedom I seek

Can You Forgive Yourself?

Can you forgive yourself?
Forgive yourself for the disenfranchising deeds
You caused yourself
Or others caused
Can you see the wisdom-gain if you did?
Or are you blind to it?
Blinded by your own victimization of yourself
All these things can change if you let them
What are the sins put against you?
By yourself and others
Are they worth holding onto?
Or are they just holding you back?
I suspect you think it's safer this way
You don't have to think
You don't have to self challenge
You don't have to work at it
You don't have to change, everyone else does
Are they not just scapegoats?
Scapegoats to your self medicating demise
It's easier to live a life of spent dreams
Than it is to change the things that need changing
Are you sure?
I say not
It's far easier to let go
Let go, and forgive yourself and others
Than to carry the pain for forever and a day
When you forgive
Life gets lighter to live
And what of the wisdom gained by forgiveness?
Is your enlightenment that you will live a truer, freer and softer life?
Then you ever thought possible
No longer a victim of yourself

But a victor of yourself and the ones that follow your lead
So, these questions remain
Can you forgive yourself?
Can you learn from the wisdom of forgiving yourself?
Can you stop being your own worst victimizing enemy?
Can you be grateful in doing so?
Becoming who you were meant to be
Self forgiving, ever wiser
A victor of past misgivings and self neglect
Living the life you always wanted to have
Answer the questions
And you will see
Your fullest potential that can be

"Give onto others from your heart
But, do not expect the same in return
For it is in that you give
But your own reservations towards others
By that you know you have given but yourself
Do not give more then you have to offer
Because it will cause you more pain
Rather then the joy of giving"

Children of Tomorrow

The children you birth and raise
Are not your children
For they are the world's children
It is through today's children that tomorrow will begin
So do not control these children
But rather guide them
Guide then with your positives
And not your negatives
For if you do
There will be no change from today's negatives
And will only bring more pain and sorrow upon tomorrow's world
Guide them with sweet countenance
And never raise thy staff in vain
But rather with purpose of guiding redirection
From our present world's misdirection
For if you inflict pain on the world's children
You will only mar tomorrow's achievements
Listen
Listen to the children
Hear what they are saying
And hear what they are not saying
For in that you may learn where we went wrong
Wisdom comes in many forms
So listen
For your staff that you may use against your children
May actually be your wings that set you free?
So listen to the children carefully
They are tomorrow's beginning
And tomorrow's hope
From as we are today, impediment to humanity's development
They are tomorrow's forthcoming

With the dreams we once had
The dreams of change and chance
That they can be better and bring better
For their world
The world of tomorrow
The children you bear
Are not your children
But rather the world's children
So guide them well
Listen to them often
For without guiding and listening to the children well
Will only prevent the world's children from achieving their goals
Their goals of hope and a chance of a better world
Where we have failed
However do not hold the children on a pedestal
For it will not advance the future of tomorrow
But rather will perpetuate the continuous incestuous retardation of
    the world
And dash the hopes that they can change our wrongs
Because they were cherished and not taught well
The children you birth and raise
Are not your children
For they are the world's children
So do not control these children
But rather guide them well
For today's children are tomorrow's beginning
And it is only in the eyes of the children's children
That we will see if there is a change
A change of betterment that truly happens
So guide the children well
For they are our hopes of tomorrow
Hopes we become better people
And inclusive of all mankind
Guide our children well
Do not put a negative mark on them

So they can have the life we as children once dreamt of
The children you birth and raise
Are not your children
They are forevermore the world's children

"Our spirituality defines us
We grow though it
As well as others!"

Crime and Punishment

Tell us of crime and punishment
What can I tell you of crime and punishment?
When one commits a crime against one of us
He does not just commit a crime against the victims
He commits a crime on all of us
Including himself
And the punishment he receives
Is punishment upon all of us?
If I hurt you
I do not just hurt you
I hurt myself
And all in the world
For the pain I suffer is everyone's pain
If I share joy with you
The whole world feels our joy
It is Creator's way of telling us we are all connected
When you throw a pebble upon the water
Does it not ripple?
As with every action does it not have a reaction?
As with the criminal
We are criminals also
For not understanding what lead him to that event
And not providing him opportunities to become more
Before the crime was committed
We are not just responsible for our own being
But for all of man
And our punishment for his shortcomings
Is the punishment incurred to us by his needs unmet?
Though we walk through life as individuals
We are all one

With no distinction from another
With the realization of our own shortcomings
Are we not all criminals needing to be punished?
For not understanding our need for each other
For crime and punishment only provides us with a view of our own
    short sightedness

A lady said
"Where are all the good men?"
I said
"We are out there. We sometimes hide under rocks like an ogre or a
shrew waiting to be discovered and accepted by the oh so chosen few."

Do Not Eat From the Tree of Knowledge

Do not eat from the tree of knowledge
For you might learn of sin and pleasure
Joy and deceit
And yes' pain
We are kept away from this tree of knowledge
By people of control
Who twist our being
As we not need to know
And ourselves by letting them have control over us
These few
These oh so self chosen few
Who think they can have control over our free thought
Will try and keep us from eating from the tree of knowledge
Because they do not want us to learn more
More knowledge then the pig slop they feed
They deny free thought
Free thought of life and God
Pain and pleasure
Joy and deceit
They deny our free will to think and choose
They use fear and deceit
To keep us away from the tree of knowledge
And its oh so sweet fruit
Yes, they deny us our belief in God the way we see fit
And feed us rhetoric about their cloak and dagger shows
By things written by falsehoods of men
And man's false beliefs of God
Whatever that may be
They do not want us to see
The truths the tree of knowledge has to offer
Let alone letting it grow within us

If we let this knowledge grow from the tree within us
The ones that lead us with their control
Begin to lose their grip of deceit upon us
We will begin to see these controllers as demons of darkness
Holding us back from learning about ourselves as human beings
    unto ourselves
Human beings free and able to think for themselves
Not needing to have these false priests of control thinking for us
Eating from the tree of knowledge
Allows us to pick up our own shield of truth
And faith in ourselves
To decide and defend us from the deceit
The deceit of those controlling false priests
That keep life and God's truths from us
So eat from the tree of knowledge
And learn its truths
Then
But only then
Mark what ye has heard

"I am not ashamed of my God
 Nor afraid of his wrath
Because he will only do what is just for me
For he is my only judge
And dismiss the disbelieving naysayers
That pass judgement on my physical being
Because in the end it is my spiritual being
That will be judged by my God
And that is all that matters"

Do You Understand Love?

I love you!
You do?
Yes, I do!
Do you love yourself?
No! Maybe! I don't know! Sort of!
So, if you don't love yourself
How can you say I love you or love another?
For love is not a word, thing or action
But, a belief onto yourself
The essence of love comes from within
Knowing you are the best you can be
With all your goodness
And, all your bad
For you should not shun parts of you that you do not like
But rather rejoice in them
Because they are a part of you
For they are not flaws in you
But rather, beauty marks put there by your journey through life
Rejoice in them
For you would not be in the greatness of who you are without them
We beat ourselves the worst
And this self rejection hurts more then a whip in the hands of
another!
Yes, the truth be told, I was once like you
Not being loving of myself
Thinking I could love another
I had to search deep within
Within the dark recesses of my mind
To weed out and deal with
The sins of others passed onto me that I internalized
I had to deal with the sins I passed judgement onto myself with
And it hurt to look at me
It hurt so bad

To find out I was flawed to the eyes of another and myself
I looked, as you are now, for love in all the wrong ways, places and
     faces
And, not understanding it
Hurting people along the way
 Because, the feel good only lasted but a moment in time
Only to find after many years of searching and suffering
The love I sought was me
It was only then I found out what love is
It is that treasure chest I sought and found
My internal light and yes my God
I was searching to love myself
For now I can say I love you and know it's true
Love is acceptance of yourself
The unsheathing of the masks that bind us
This unsheathing of ourselves is the awaking of our new
     understanding of love
The love that is not forced
Is the one that is true
Now, do you understand why I questioned your love for me?
What are you going to do?
If you look at yourself you may not like it
But without it you will never know what love is
Oh, but if you do and you accept you
You will experience pure light radiating from you
For then you found your love and your God
But if you cannot face the shadows of your past
To feel true love
You will walk through life with a continued emptiness upon your
     heart
And will not know love's joy, and wonderment
But, only know love's torment
I do understand, it is hard work
If you won't face the challenge to love yourself
Please don't tell me you love me or another
Until you can look at yourself and say I love you
Oh, so incredible me

But, just remember I do love you!
For you the way you are
So, for me to know that you love me
Without looking away
Or your face buried in a hug
You're going to have to be able say I love you
Looking at me in the eye
Smiling at me
Then I will know that you love me
Because you love yourself
And are free to truly love others
Now do you understand what love is?

Don't Lose Yourself in Yourself

Stop thinking so much
Don't lose yourself in yourself
Come out
Stay out
Stay out to live and play
You have more to offer yourself and others
If you stay out and play
In the here and now
So, please don't retreat
Retreat to your inner mind
It isn't fine
When you're in your mind
All the time
So, come out and live and play
In the world of the here and now
Be with me, don't analyze me
Be free with me
So you can see
That we need you
To be free of your imprisoning self
So we can live a life
A life of honesty and integrity together
So, don't lose yourself in yourself
Be mindful of the retreat to your inner self
Respect it
But, stay here with me
Because I want and accept you, oh so lovely you
For who and why you are
And for the way you are
So, don't retreat into your inner self
I don't want you to analyze me

And everything you see
So, come out and stay out with me
I don't want to lose you to yourself
So, don't lose yourself in yourself
Come and spend a life with me
If you can't come out of your head for me
Then find a new friend and come out of yourself with them
For someone as beautiful as you
Should not lose yourself in yourself
Come out and be yourself for yourself
And be free like the wind upon yourself

Eating and Drinking

Eat well and drink well
But know what you're eating and drinking
Be willing to break bread with those less fortunate
For then you will always feel full
Drink and be merry
But share your joy
For the world will smile with gratitude
When you have a full belly
Don't just groan that you ate too much
But rather be grateful that you ate
For others may not even see food to eat
Be thankful for the ones who toil in the soil
And put food on your table
For without them, you would grow lean in your existence
When you drink
Thank with praise of the blood and sweat it took to make your wine
And give thanks once again for the ones that laboured to make it
For without them you would die of thirst
In doing these small gestures
You will become a wiser, more thankful, and giving man
Understanding the need for all weathers
And all people
For without them you would not have a full belly
Wine in your glass
And a song of merriment upon your lips

Excuses

What excuses are you going to use today?
The excuses we use are the excuses we use
We all use excuses for whatever reason
But why do we use them?
Should we use them?
What are we hiding by using them?
Is the truth too hard to bear?
Why can't we speak the truth?
Have we sinned too much to ever speak the truth?
Or is our truth really our sin?
What will happen if we stop the excuses and tell the truth?
Would the truth really condemn us?
Or will the truth make us whole?
We lie to the people around us with excuses
We lie to ourselves with the very same excuses
Why can't we ever tell the truth?
Why must we always lie?
Using excuses
Excuses that only hinder us
From being true to ourselves
And being true to the ones we love
Let alone the countless others in our lives
Are we that afraid of ourselves?
To show our truths
Instead of an excuse
Talk about self abuse
When we hide our truths behind an excuse
Every minute we live is borrowed time
Time that is wasted by lying excuses
Isn't our time here on this earth worth the truth?
Excuses behold only uneasy truths in time
When are we going to stop the excuses?
And get real

Real with ourselves
Real with everyone else
The truth be told
There's no time for excuses
There's no time for half truths
Because time is ticking
Our end is nearing
Isn't it time to stop the excuses?
And tell the truth
If we want more out of ourselves, others and our lives
Excuses are killing our quality time
Our quality time here on earth
Excuses are killing who we really are
It's time to get real
And be real
Without the excuses that are keeping us from experiencing ourselves
Isn't it better to live a life worth living?
Being true to ourselves and others
Think about it
Excuses are keeping us from ourselves
Our true authentic selves
Or, does seeing who you really are scar you?
Are you that afraid to show your real self?
That you'd rather waste time
 To live a false life
Lying and hiding behind excuses
Excuses are not real but merely a scapegoat
A scapegoat from living an authentic you
So if you can't live with the real you
I guess you're bound to live a questionable life
Lying and hiding behind your needless excuses

What of Freedom?

What of freedom?
What of it I say?
What freedom do you speak of?
Freedom as set out by man with his laws and decrees
Or your own freedom of self control and decision
Tell us of both
My question to you is, are you truly free?
With laws set forth by man
And with your being
Seeing all with your mind's eye
Under man's dear prudence you will never know freedom
For man takes great joy in controlling your freedom with laws
I am not talking about laws that prevent man from harming one
    another
Even though our leaders break the same laws they set
I speak of the laws and decrees that prevent us from living free
To just be
We seek structure from the ones we appoint to lead us
Yet they only find ways to control us
Where is the freedom in that?
Man has never ever known freedom
Freedom from man's cruelty, religious persecution, control, and greed
So there is no freedom amongst men
Only more control
Now I ask, are you free inside yourself?
For most are bound to belief in the laws and decrees as set out by
    others
And behave in the manor that reflects this
Thus forsaking any true look at one's own being
Where freedom truly lies

It is only through understanding and accepting of oneself one will
   truly be free
And man will never know freedom until he does
This freedom is not an external event
But an internal awareness that self and knowing man can change
You can choose to go through life believing what you are told
Guided by inept leaders and legislators
Hating other men and ways
Be controlling of others
And have harmful greed by nature
Or you can look at yourself and listen to your mind's eye and know
   freedom
For with better understanding and acceptance of thyself will freedom
   reign
Men will question this thought about freedom
And say we live in a free society
But I say not when laws abound
Abound with no direction but control
So accept and understand yourself
For it is the only true freedom you will ever have
For man only seeks to control man
And freedom will only reign in your heart, mind, and soul
Then you will know freedom
For it will be the only freedom you will ever know

"We spend a lifetime trying to become whole. But, it is only upon
our death that we are finally there."

Friends

Friends
Friends are the stepping stones of your development
They see you in your becoming
And know were you have been
You learned from them
And taught the same
True friends know when you're weak
And will be your pillar of strength unannounced to you when needed
And not ask for anything in return
Except your continued friendship
They take not from you more then they need
To strengthen your kinship
And respect your decisions along your journey together
Though they may not like them
They respect them anyway
Friends will be each other's mentors and guides
Loving each other without condition
True friends will come and go for half a lifetime
But will pick up the conversation where they left off
In that you know you have a true friend
May you always praise your unfailing friends with love and
    faithfulness
With your honour and undying respect
Because true friends are hard to find
And are few and far between
Cherish your true friends
And weigh caution on the ones who only know you in passing
They may say that they're your friends
But they are leaches on your graces

Nevertheless
Take from them
Of what you need
And move on quickly
As to not diminish your being

Give Me a Reason

Give me a reason
Give me a reason to show myself
I'll give you a reason not to
People don't want to see you for you
For it distorts their perceived notion of who you are
And gives them a reason to chastise you
So, give me a reason to show myself
People don't want to see you for who you are
They won't be able to accept me
If they see me for who I am
For the ones that do see me
Accept me with reserve
Because I'm not their idea
So, give me a reason to show myself
The road of life is long
Without unconditional love and acceptance
Give me a reason
Give me a reason to be myself
Give me a reason to stay
Without acceptance why stay
When the road of life is long
And it is easier to grab my pack and go
Travel the road and give and receive love superficially
And only show a part of me
The hale fellow well meet part of me
It is what people want
So, give me a reason
One good reason to show you who I am
I bet you can't handle it
So, give me a reason
It's easier to walk on

Than to deal
Walking on is predicable and to me understandable
Dealing is the risk
I'd rather walk on
Then to see the deal
It isn't worth the risk
So, give me a reason to stay
And feel the negative pain
The pain of rejection for who or why I am
It's easier to walk on
Than to deal with the dealt pain of your rejection
For showing you who I am
I just know I don't want the pain
The pain of your shallowness
So, give me a reason
A reason to show you me
Will you accept me?
It's easier to walk on
From the perceived pain of your ridicule
With that I don't have a reason
A reason to show you who I am
So, I'll just grab my pack and walk on now
Unless you can give me a reason to stay

I Am Half the Man I Used To Be

I am half the man I used to be
But yet, I am more of a man then I ever was
Twisted life
Turning time
Always trying to find our divine
But time passes
And we're still sitting on our asses
And now wearing glasses
Nothing we find seems fine
Turning time
Twisted life
I worked and loved hard and paid the price
Busted body
Broken hearted
I'm half the man I used to be
But wiser then I have ever been
Wisdom well earned
But some gained with distain
Other wisdom earned left a life stain
And some wisdom gained caused major pain
It was not in vain
Because of the wisdom gain
I am half the man I used to be
But yes, I am more of the man than I ever was
Twisted life
Turning time
I am older now and have wisdom to share
Some of the wisdom gained still has pain
But that's OK
I lived a life
I lived my life

The way it was to be
Twisted time
Turning life
I am half the man I used to be
But, I am a wiser man then I ever was
And will ever be
For now

I Long For a Time Gone By

I long for a time gone by
When the men were strong
And the women mighty
When the rush wasn't there
And the focus was survival or despair
When the winds blew cold
And the houses seemed colder
When we relied on family
And had a sense of community
Yes, the times were harder
We had to work for it
It was hard and well earned work
Instead of it served to us on a golden platter
That seems to make us only get fatter
I long for a time gone by
When it all seemed simpler
And family mattered
And we relied on the community
When we were in a moment of despair
There were fewer laws
And we lived true
True to our own self-developed moral rules
Our advances in this world
Only deprive us of our chance to live
Live with our true nature of ourselves
Where we lived and counted on our instincts to survive
And be better men
I long for a time gone by
When things were simpler
And seemed freer
And we valued the time spent with our fellow man
I long for those days gone by

I Seek the Truth

Come off thy mountain
To speak to me
Show me that you are real
Show me that your words are true
Show me that the words written are true
Cause I grow weary
Of the rhetoric of man
Saying that is written is true
I am not of the chosen ones
To lead or follow blindly
I must see the truth
And the sins of reason to believe
To learn the pain of knowing too much
Or blindness by not knowing enough
Am I a fool to seek the truth?
Or a wise man unbeknownst to myself?
If you are there, come off of your mountain and speak to me
I grow weary of these doomsayers and false priests
Telling me that you are so
I believe you to be
Just not the way they say you are
One false priestess saying you are this way
And another false priest saying you are that way
Frankly, I think you are laughing at mankind
You created the idea of you
Only for mankind to taint the true image and meaning of you
Because mankind is increasingly controlling, greedy, manipulative,
    and maladaptive
Retarded you may say
The image of you is supposed to be good

But mankind has perverted you
For their own unjust deeds
So come off thy mountain
To speak to me
Show me that you are real to me
Then I will follow the true you
And not what man has made you to be for them
 I grow weary of the rhetoric of man
Simpletons to the end
You were here long before man knew how to write
Guiding us through the spirit world
Referring to you as Creator of all kind
Yet you taught man to write
Was this for you to amuse yourself?
With the division of mankind
In the mistaken writings of man
I think I hear you laughing
It is a joke
How as children of God we destroy each other in your name
So, oh great one
Creator of all living things
Come off thy mountain
And speak to me
Show me that you are real
Show me that your words are true
Cause I grow weary
Of the rhetoric of man
And I seek the truth

I Was Just Standing In My Power

I guess I was just standing in my power
Just trying to please another
What a waste of energy
What a waste of time
Or was it?
I did learn from it
I learned about lies
I learned about half truths
I learned about acceptance
I learned that I should not always have to defend who I am
Why I am
Or, the way I am
To anyone but myself
I guess I was just standing in the way of my power
For trying to please another
Zapping my energy
From my magnetic synergy
I'll have to choose someone less finicky
Someone who is willing to accept me the way I am
One not looking for the idea whim
Was I just standing in my power?
Just trying to please another
Or, was I just standing up for my power by going through the process
So, I could learn from it
I don't know for sure
It's not all a blur
But I do know I will not defend who I am to anyone again
Accept me for who I am
Or don't

I rightfully don't care
Because I'm not going to try to please another
When it will stand in the way of my power
Anyone who wants to be with me will have to accept me
Accept me the way I am
And not use excuses as to why or why not
For I or anyone else will never stand in my power again
And so it is

I Was Put Here For a Purpose

I am not of this world
And I am not long in this world
I was put here for a purpose
I do not know what that is yet
When it is foreseen to me
I will act
Act
Act with dignity and honour
To fill the purpose of my being
As I am not long to this world
And I must fill my life task
Before I leave this world
Creator will show me thy purpose when the time is right
It may be a vision or a light
It may be an eagle or a hawk
That will talk
While I sit on a rock
Listening to the wind and the wave
For it was Creator who truly gave
Herself to man
But man is lacking to understand
What their purpose is here
We no longer share
And only cause despair
Thinking it's fair
Destroying Mother Earth
Thinking this is their purpose here
I am just waiting now
Waiting to be shown my purpose
Creator will show me when the time is right
The answer then will be in plain sight
She may use the tortoise or the hare as the sign
Either way whatever the sign

It will be fine
My purpose for being here will be shown in due time
Creator and Mother Earth knows best
And soon will put me to the test
The test to fulfill my purpose here
I await for the sign
I am not long in this world
And I was put here to fulfill a purpose
That Creator wants me to do
I wait with my ever wandering soul
For the sign
Of Creator's design
That will guide me to complete my purpose here on earth
For I am not of this world
And I am not long in this world
I was put here for a purpose
A purpose I must fulfill
Before I leave this earth
I await the sign
That will be set out by design
For me to find
I was put here for a purpose
Without it what was the purpose of my birth

Relationship Vision Statement

My partner, my lover, and my best friend shall live together with dedication and commitment to each other. Allowing each other to be true to ourselves, to pursue our dreams and aspirations as individuals or a couple. We will not allow ourselves to stand in each others shadow. We as individuals, in our commitment to each other be but one pillar of our temple together. For in that our love will be fluid and alive!

I'm Sorry, Thank You, With Love

To the lady I once had the opportunity to love
I am sorry for my misgivings
From the irrational thoughts of pain
That created pain on you
I am sorry for each and every hurt I bore
For it had nothing to do with you
But my own misunderstanding of myself
And the pain I was in
I forgive all things you may have done or not done
Because I finally forgave myself
Of past sins I put on myself
Your beauty will forever remain part of my heart
I will not forget
But honour
The good that happened in our togetherness
For it was you
That started me on my healing journey
With the love you gave me
And I honour, respect, and will never forget that love
And I truly love you for that
You gave me strength
When I least expected it
And you still give me strength to this day
Every time I think of you
Warm feelings eclipse my heart and a smile comes to my face
I'll be forever in your debt
For the love you gave
The love we shared
Because without you
And that action that ended our togetherness
I would have never become who I am today
I only regret is that you will never see who I became

We were great together then
We would have been magic now
If I only knew then
What I know now
I just want you to know I still love you
And it was an honour to have had you in my life
For you helped make me a great man
And I am extremely proud to have had you in my life
As I am just as proud of who you became
Through it all
I forgive you
Because I forgave myself
I am sorry for all the hurt I caused
I thank you for loving me
I thank you for leaving me
For it allowed me to become a better man
By learning to love myself
And I will always honour and love you for that and more
Until we meet again

Inspiring Excitement

What excites you?
What inspires you?
About life's new possibilities
That you see
By looking within
Ahh
Is it, no more feelings of emptiness within?
The feeling of being whole
Contentment with yourself
Of who you become
With no more need to drink rum
 And act dumb
Are you now inspired?
Inspired by the one looking back in the looking glass
And not needing others to inspire you
There's nothing like being your own inspiration
Instead of self ridicule of indecision
The power within is incredible
And you're not indebted to others
For you now see greatness
Your greatness
In the past you have been what has been
Nervous of being
Aggressive to cover up
Engaged in little
And disengaged in lots
Now this has changed
You are no longer disengaged from living your life
And are in the land of the living
Isn't it wonderful?
Being more then you have ever been before

Bet you never thought before
That life could be more then a chore
Or even a bore
Here's to living
Living an exciting inspiring life
So what are the exciting inspirations you are going to have of yourself
today?

Interesting

Interesting
I am such a weight on another
Separation will make us stronger
Interesting
I'm too heavy a person
For them to handle
Interesting
When they sought me out
For answers they were seeking
Of themselves
Interesting
Cause I did my job
For them to question themselves
Only for them to run away from their answers
Of themselves
Interesting
For everything I brought up
Were observations I saw in them
Was a reflection of me
Interesting
So they ran
Saying I was too heavy
To be their friend
Interesting
Because they chose me
Only to reject themselves
By saying we can't be friends right now
Until we are stronger
Interesting
The projection one puts out to protect oneself
Interesting
As long as it is on their terms
The weight of any friendship

Interesting
I guess I've done my job too well
Or not well enough
Because they ran
From the gifts they asked of me
Interesting
How seekers are runners
When the truth is before them
Interesting
If they did not want to know more why did they seek me out?
Interesting
Because I will always make them question
Who and why they are
So why do they seek me out
Only to run from what is real
Interesting
I think I'll stop putting myself out there
So people don't seek me for their answers
Life is too short to be lonely
After they run away
Saying I'm too heavy for them to handle
Interesting
It is much easier to sit here and write about things
While drinking a bottle of rum
To feel numb
From my rum
Then it is to feel numb
After people run
For only giving them what they were seeking in the first place
Aspects of themselves
Interesting
I'm too heavy now
So I'll just drink some rum
And lose the weight
Interesting

Humans are interesting creatures
But man, can they ever be a pain
Oh, how interesting

"Beauty is in the eyes of the beholders
In that, love will flourish and be true.
For what anyone else thinks of it, doesn't matter
They are not you!"

It's Your Choice

It's your choice
It's your responsibility
To change for yourself
Will your choice empower you?
Or will it keep you stuck in the same?
So you can play the game
That keeps you in shame
Or will you empower yourself?
And take responsibility for the self-imposed game
The game that allows you to victimize yourself
The game that holds you back
That same game that gives you flack
Each time you think you're going forward
You end up two steps back
It's time
It's time to deal with it
But you can't
It's yours
And you don't want to let go
You're afraid
You're afraid you might lose yourself
If you let go
Let go of the crap
That's holding you back
Yes, I know you're used to it being in your ruck sack
But it's like sitting on a tack
Causing you more distain
And lots of pain
It's your choice
It's your responsibility
What are ya going to do?
Are you going to take the risk?
The risk of responsibility to change

Are you going to empower yourself to change the same old game?
It's your fame
Or not
It's up to you
Live with the old goo
Or move on to a better you
Without your past poo
What is your choice?
And are you going to be responsible enough to change?
Because your disempowering patterns and habits are easier to follow
And change is hard to do
Empowering yourself means change
It means work
It means self commitment to become more
What are you going to do?
Be more
Or stand still
Like a picture never changing fixed in time
And that would be a crime
Either way you're going to have to live with it
It's your choice

"We were all runners
Only to seek ourselves in the end"

Joy and Sorrow

Joy and sorrow are one and the same
For they are cut from the same cloth
And you cannot have one without the other
For what causes you joy
Will ultimately cause you sorrow
And what you sorrow about
Will in the end cause you joy
I understand a doubter's doubt
Saying they are not
And joy is greater then sorrow
But joy and sorrow are woven together as one
And always have been and always will be
There is great joy in love's delight
And there is great sorrow in love's ending
Through this sorrow we learn
Grow
And feel
The joy of love's longing for itself
As we find the joy in loving another once again
You may ask
How do you find joy in the sorrow of one's death?
Death should not be a sorrowful occasion
But rather a joyous one
For he who shone upon your life and this earth
Has lived
That alone should be joyous
Because he contributed to your life by living
Now he contributes to your life by dying
So you have a reason to move on
And that is joyous as well

Joy and sorrow will always be inseparable
Though you may feel them separate
The other waits quietly until needed
In the end and together
Joy and sorrow will be there to start a new day

Know Thy Truth upon Thyself

Will all of us who know the truths
Of the doomsayers and false priests
Have our right
Cut out of history's wrong
Because we are naysayers of mass ignorance
And illogical thought processes of control
Of the ones who dictate their untruths as truths to us
Why must we bide by these edicts of ignorance?
Proclaiming their religions is the one and only truth
And we must abide by the laws set forth by similar ignorant edicts
Who dictate all our other free thought and will
Will mankind always fall and bow down to stupidity of control?
Or will we have our chance to live
To seek our own spiritual journey
To decide from our right and wrong
And seek our own moral development
Without these edicts of elsewhere and false priests dictating to us
We seek no more or no less then life's longing of itself
To learn and listen to nature and man
Set out by nature itself
The highest clergy
Man should not fear the unknown as set out by other men
Nor, should they be bound by laws
Laws that retard their very nature of curiosity and self decision
But seek all truths unto themselves
There is no freedom in the world
When man controls man
These doomsayers and false priests will not allow that freedom
And those of us who know the truths
Will be cast out
Depicted as ill
Or locked up

In order to protect the false words and laws of control bound ignorant
    men
What if there is no promised land
Nor garden of Eden
Or heaven
As they dictate their false truths at us
But rather just maybe
An equal plane of existence and acceptance for all mankind and their
    spirits
Until mankind can lie down those words as said by the doomsayers
    and false priests
We will be bound to live to the end of time with torment and turmoil
And those of us who know the truths
Will only know thy truths upon thy self
Because there is no place left to hide
From these edicts of elsewhere, doomsayers and false priests
Only when we destroy ourselves
Will man see them as the charlatans they were
Do not be bound by what other men have said
Know yourself well enough
To know thy truths upon thyself
Only then ye shall have lived
And truly know freedom

Live like a Kid's King

Isn't life a process to live to your fullest?
We seem to forget this as we grow old
Conforming to the indecisions of man
We were once kids
And were free thinkers
But which was taken away by the conformities of now
Life has changed
We can no longer think or be free
I once lived like a kid's king
Thinking and being free
Free to make my own moral decisions of life
But know we must bide by rule cloaked in deceit
What of just moral men
Why must we heed those of you cloaked in moral deceit?
Making ridiculous rules to protect their immoral deeds
What happened to whoever lives by the truth will die with it in his
    heart
How can we live life to the fullest?
Conforming to immoral rules created by immoral men
I lived like a kid's king once
Seeing and living life
Through big eyes of wonderment and excitement
Wonderment and excitement that allowed me to learn and grow
And opened my eyes to my heart
Now by the stupidity of man it has become a challenge
A challenge to make my own right moral decision
A decision without being chastised
Chastised by those who serve a lesser God
One cloaked in moral deceit and control
Living by rules of self limitation and ignorance
Conform, conform, conform!
How will man ever evolve?
If he can not accept

Accept that things do happen for reasons
Reasons unannounced to them
By the Gods that be
And that no rule will ever change that
Rules are made to control you
To feed someone's greed
Or to console someone's uneasy conscience
What of just moral men
I was a free thinker once
Living like a kid's king
Not thinking or acting like a king of kids
Controlling every move you make
Sometimes it's the simplest thought
The simplest action
That is the best rule
The best moral action
I lived like a kid's king once
Seeing and living life
Through big eyes of wonderment and excitement
Wonderment and excitement that allowed me to learn and grow
And opened my eyes to my heart
I long for that so!

Brain Fog

My brain Fog is making me feel like a drained dog
It's like trying to walk on a bog
I don't have much energy so I'll just sit on that log
My brain feels like I'm looking through eggnog
It' makes my thoughts sound like a croaking Bullfrog
It's a pain like cleaning a drain clog
Oh that damn brain fog
My mind is like French toast and syrup all sog
I can't get my fat ass off of this log
Because of that brain fog
I guess I have to forget about riding my hog
And just sit on this log
Cursing that damn brain fog

Madman in Tow

Who's that intruder looking at you?
Oh no! it's your madman in tow
What have you done?
What didn't you do?
What did someone do to you?
Boohoo
Why is your madman looking at you?
Is your guilt playing on you?
Did your ego get its panties in a knot?
Your mind's getting bad thoughts
What are you going to do?
Let him through and control you
Or will you control the madman looking at you?
We all have the bad thoughts of fraught
It's all based on how you were taught
Or not
Ego hurt
Madman can exert
What are you going to do?
It's about who's controlling who
The madman will cost you more than you know
Life balance is living with your madman in tow
Good virus evil
White wolf versus black wolf
What are you doing to do?
And to who?
Because it is truly only about you
Are you going to give your life a screw?
For you, life spent, might be locked in a room the size of a shoe
Living your life with moth balls in your head
And always seeing red
Or will you choose
Choose to live in balance

With the madman in tow only in your head
To give you strength
In moments of weakness
So as not to be victims
Victims to other madmen in tow
The madman can ruin your life
Or save it
It is about balance
Living with the madman in tow

My Spirit Guide

Years ago I dreamt of a wise elder floating horizontally only to fall
into nothingness. I did not see him again until I carved his face
unintentionally. That's why I called the carving Spirit Guide.

Make Your Death Worth Your Birth

The only cause of death is birth
So live life for what it's worth
And speak only your truth
Onto yourself
For in the end it is your truth
That will measure your truest worth
To yourself and your maker
So if you want to live life as a taker
And a faker
Your Creator will be your foresaker
And will be thy maker
Of your eternal outcome
We may not always live life with the truest hearts
And life is very much the living arts
Always wielding,
Changing
Rearranging
With new staging
The only cause of death is birth
So live life for what it's worth
And speak only your truth
Make your life worth living
Don't just live a life
For just a life lived is living strife
Reach out and become more
So your life's truths are not a bore
Or just looking for a score
For then life is truly a chore
Don't live life with other's calluses sore
Because there is so much more
When we see and speak our truths
We discover our worth
And live a life worth living

And not just a life lived
We were born for a reason
Live and speak the truths you were truly given
So become your most
And speak your truest truths
So live your life to the fullest
And make your death worth your birth

Maybe We Have To Let It Get Messed Up Before We Can Step Up

Maybe we have to let it get messed up before we can step up
We all have a dark side
Can you accept mine?
My dark side helps me process what I messed up
So accept it
Understand I don't need another judge judging may own self
    judgements
I'm hard enough on myself as it is
And I know I cannot avoid dealing with the mess up
I've just got to fess up
To the mess up
And move on
One good thing about looking in on the dark side
I'm willing to go back and work on what I screwed up
So I can learn form it
Grow
And move on
What about you?
Can you?
Can you step up to what you messed up?
Does your dark side help you fix what you messed up?
I can and will accept you the way you are
Because I will not pass judgement on you
You'll judge yourself enough for all parties concerned
You've just got to fess up
To the mess up
Deal with it
And move on

So what have we learned from this little misadventure
 Maybe we have to let it get messed up before we can step up
So we can grow

"When you test your fate with stupidity
You are bound to pay a price
But, if your fate is accidentally met
The price paid will be the lesser
Even with the same outcome"

Med Dishing

The chemicals in my head are swishing
And I don't want another round of pill dishing
That keeps me wishing
My head be not a-swishing
But the doctors keep a-dishing
I almost think he's a-pushing
Because my heads a-rushing
Man, do I feel like flushing
Them damn pills he's pushing
You have the mind a-mushing
Street person pushing
Seeking minds hushing
But your mind remains rushing
And crazily swishing
Let's have another round of pill dishing
Dishing the chemical culture of classification
What of mind formation?
Or do we sit on our thumbs and apply rotation
And blow mind formation
Bowing to the notion of chemical culture classification
Oh my head is a-swishing
And the street dealer and the doctor a-pushing
My brain is oozing and a-pussing
Why am I a-fussing?
What's the mater with feeling like a fistulas pussing?
That good old mind a-mushing
And life a-rushing
Like a toilet flushing
My mind has been hushed
Mushed
And flushed
In the attempts to get better
The cure is worse then the illness

With that chemical culture classification
My mind is now rushing
I'm going to get sick now
So I'm going to go rushing
And do some flushing
As my mind is a-rushing
But will I make it
Because my gait
Is irate
With chemical culture classification

Moving On

The ice is forming in the river now
The last of the stubborn leaves finally went with the wind
As fall fades and the cold winter winds begin to blow
It is time, I have the itch to go
Onward to a more distant land
To a land I loved in my youth
And have been in my dreams ever since
For then, I will be truly home
I stopped here in the land of my youth to heal
For I was wounded by love's crucifixion
The wind blows cold and I must go
My homeland calls
A childhood friend is saddened by my short stay
But understands my love for my homeland
As with the winter wind
She knows I must go
As I gear up to move on, I am torn
For I have found someone to bleed willingly and open with
One that, I wish would join me on love's dance floor
But she is in another distant land
And like me has been wounded by love's crucifixion and needs time
    to heal
I am torn
For we are both wanting to go home to our homeland
But she remains pestered by love's crucifixion
And must stay, for now, in the land of her torment
For that I am torn
In time, I hope we can be together
Together on love's dance floor
For I am willing, if she is
But only when she's ready
The winds blow colder now
And I must trudge on

My Dear Lady Thank You

Oh, my dear lady
You have touched my heart
You have touched my soul
With joy and wonderment
You have given me hope
For the future
And disdain for my past actions
But joy of resolution with them
To walk freely in mind and body
Knowing my future is not more of my past
To walk strong and free with conviction
Of my presence
The Presence that has been always there
But I let others play with and take from me
Because I was weak
And could not speak
Speak up and say no
I am not going to let anyone take
What's rightfully mine anyway
My Spirit and my soul
No control
Will be held over me ever again
Oh, my dear lady
You have touched my heart
You have touched my soul
Because you helped me
Find my inner voice
To stop the self-victimization
And to say no
To the takers
And the fakers
Who I let identify me instead of myself
Takers of easy pray

And the doers of devilish deeds
To hold me down
So they had control
Control over me
Saying, I can't, I am not, you will not
Because you're not much of a person
But a muse
So we can abuse
Oh, my dear lady
Thank you for accepting me
Challenging me
Not accepting what I thought of me
Oh, my dear lady
You have my heart and soul
For showing me a better way
To my inner self
So I can be true to and with myself
So I can rightfully receive
My place in this world
Being whole
Not no longer being held back
By my oh so twisted thinking
That I let others help create
Now I can go forth
And seek out
My true direction
In my destiny
With a new outlook on life
All proud and strong
Showing my positives
And not being limited to my negatives
Oh, my dear lady
You have my heart and soul
Because you helped me find my self-worth and self-love
So others can see investing in me
Is worth the effort
To give life's riches and love

Oh, my dear lady
Thank you
With all my heart
For showing me a better way
A better way of seeing and being myself
My dear lady
You have my heart, with love

North By North East I Will Seek My Way

North by northeast I will seek my way
There is nothing here in this barren land of concrete and glass
My mental heart is with the wind
Like the water never wanting to settle and be still
Seeking out opportunities of nay
Looking for that better place to stay
A place out around the bay?
Garr
But maybe Narr
It depends on my mental heart
If the winds and the water be still
It's been forty odd years since calm reigned
In this wayward soul
Though much loved
With same given
None have ever calmed this wind bound soul
For more then a day
North by northeast I will seek my way
There's nothing here that wants me to stay
North by northeast I will seek my way
To a windswept land
Of barren rock, bog, and stunted growth
Where fairy folk dwell
Where past generations learned to survive
With less and grew strong in their existence
It is in this barrenness I may find some calming of my soul's wind
By the land, wind, and water and that hardiness of life it provides
I my not have the truest of hearts
But I do have a right to survive

With it intact
North by northeast I will seek my way
Away from this barren land of concrete and glass
To that blessed Isle I love the best
Then I may find my hearts content
Home in my hearts delight
And if I don't
At least my heart may be at rest
North by northeast I will seek my way

Garr = great Narr = not

Ode to My Friends
(What my friends mean to me)

I have been blessed with many good friends
I would lay waste to my own heart
If I did not give honour to those friends
For my friends have honoured me
By allowing me into their hearts
Old friends see where I am
And know where I've been
New friends see where I am
And in time will know where I was
So, let our journey begin
You accepted me for who I am
You stood by me in crisis
Encouraged me when needed
Discouraged me when I should have been
Guided me when called for
Yet, you were all wise enough to let me flounder
For God and me to find the way
For that I am truly grateful
We shared, cared, laughed, and cried together
We gave hope too
And we stood tall and proud together
For that I've been honoured to be your friend
I love you all
God bless
And God's speed to some
Until we can spend time together again

Of Seagulls and Men

Have humans in the developed world become this bad
That we have become interbred with seagulls
Mine, Mine, Mine
All the time
It definitely seems that way
What happened to sharing and communal rights?
Or have our advancements propitiated our personal greed
Mine, Mine, Mine
And diminished our community togetherness and development
Mine, Mine, Mine
Greedy to take and gobble up our piece of what we think is our God
    given right
When we have not earned it
Mine, Mine, Mine
We give great honour to people no mater how they achieved it
While the ones they stepped on getting there bleed in the streets
Mine, Mine, Mine
Does this make it true then that moral man is doomed
Doomed to become no more then picked specimens of ethical man
Hidden in some dark laboratory somewhere
So the Memes of power, greed, and control can ruin what's left of
    moral man
Mine, Mine, Mine
Is mankind finished then?
To be nothing more then excrement of the memes
Always speaking mine, mine, mine
Always seeking more mine, mine, mine
Waiting for some silly arse to drop his guard so they can take what is
    his
Hush, I hear them coming now
Mine, Mine, Mine
Is the destruction of man going to be based on such lunacy?
And will we ever be able to stop it?
What of moral and just men?

On Learning

The world is full of opportunities and learning
So teach your children well
Learning is not just in the seats of a classroom
But in the whole world
With all peoples and all cultures
So do not bind the child by set rules of conformity
For then we only take away their imagination
And their willingness to seek more
Do not teach them what you think they should be taught
Or control them on how they should learn
Or not teaching what you think they should not know
Let them be free thinkers towards their learning
For a learner does not need to be taught
But rather guided towards the learning
For in the end they will learn what is needed
Ultimately when the child finds what they want to learn
Learning is no longer a chore set out by others
But rather a joy because they choose what they want to learn
Do not expect greatness in all their learning
For some will only want to learn what's needed to get by in life
Nevertheless guide these children will
Be grateful that they are learning
The ones who are learners by nature - watch them soar
They will be tomorrow's leaders
Because they guide their own path to knowledge
So set back and be there to facilitate their learning and growth
And watch the fruit of knowledge ripen
For we will all gain from the bountiful harvest
Of the learned young adult
Teach not
But rather facilitate growth
Is a learned teacher

Self Honouring Wisdom

Self honouring wisdom
We all have some
It is the inherent worth of all human beings
Give thanks for who you are
So far
Change your beliefs over time
For it will be fine
If you don't that will be your crime
Not to honour your wisdom of whom you become
Every positive has a negative
And every negative has a positive
That is your wisdom gain
Honour it
By believing in yourself
You may say you have no wisdom to honour
But I say not
For everything we know and learn is wisdom
So honour it
The stay at home parent
The abused
The disabled
The drop out
All have wisdom gained
And all have wisdom to share
It may not be in the academic sense
But one does not need academia to have wisdom
For they have lived
And that is natural wisdom
So honour it
Honour your self wisdom
For we have all been taught

And we have all been teachers
Have we not been taught by nature itself?
Our natural instincts
In that alone there is self honouring wisdom
So give honour to the wisest person you know
Yourself

Spring's New Beginning

The buds are on the trees now
The flowers are starting to bloom
And people are starting to wake from their winter hibernation
The last of the stubborn snow piles have melted away
For me I am not long here to stay
For I want to wander and play
Play in a far off distant land
To maybe take a stand
Or even just play in the sand
I just don't know
And rightfully don't care
I have no responsibilities
And not a care in the world
Spring is like a new day
Waking from its long winter's nap
Bringing new beginnings
For all to enjoy
What will I do?
Wander and play
On this beautiful spring day
Or will I take a stand and stay
For another day
Will I find what I'm looking for if I stay?
Or will I get burned by another sun ray
If I stay here and play
Man, it's hard to say
At least I don't have feet of clay
And I can find another place to play
And maybe even have a say
A say in what I want
The spring sun beats down hotter then ever
What will I do?
Spring has sprung

And I'm not sure what to do
Other than enjoy the sun
And not run
From the possibilities of a new rising spring sun
Because spring could be fun
Spring has sprung
I guess I will enjoy it and not run

Stand Up For Yourself

Are we bound to take life lying down?
Not standing up for what we want
What's in our best interest?
Not standing up against governments that protect big business and
    the rich
If you can't stand up against that
Why don't you stand up for yourself?
The one person that matters in your life, yourself
Don't use the excuses
You don't know how
You can't
Cause that's just a wash
Sure you can
Believe in yourself
It takes work
As all good things do
Aren't you worth it?
To be able to stand up for who and what you are
Stand up
Say you can
If you can't, learn how
Life is too short
To hide under a rock
Letting the world go by
To decide for you
Stand up and be counted
Deal with what's stopping you
From becoming more of you
Stop going in your shoe
Stand up and be counted
It isn't going to hurt you
You might realize it is you
Standing up for yourself

Not lying down taking the dirt
Others dish you
If you don't stand up
When people dish you
Then don't go boohoo
When you don't get what you want
Life is too short
To take it lying down
Stand up and take stock of yourself
And be counted
As a maker of change
At least a maker of your change
Lying down hasn't gotten you anywhere thus far
Stand up and be accounted for
Free yourself from your own bonds
Speak up
It's your life
Go for it
Don't take it lying down
And stand up for yourself

"Being who you are inside is your destination
Being who you are with me is all I ask
If you won't be yourself with me
Then we will never be but superficial friends
Separated by masks of deception
Created by fear and lack of understanding of yourself
Because you can't be true to yourself and with me
When wearing those masks of deception"

Stop Resisting the Resistance

Why can't you just accept it?
Why must you keep resisting?
Why must you resist the resistance by not accepting it?
Why can't you just be comfortable with the outcome?
Why do you keep using your excuses not to accept?
Can't you see it's playing on you?
By hurting you
Keeping you from becoming your most
Stop resisting the resistance
It's going to kill you
If you don't let go
Head towards the acceptance of your situation
Not the continual perpetuation of its pain
Stop resisting the resistance
It's keeping you stuck in the past
And you're going nowhere fast
The past is the past
Move on
There's more to life
When not living in the past
Can you just be with it?
Allowing your pain to be there
In the past
While allowing yourself to be here where you are
In the present
Stop resisting the resistance to change
Stop resisting the resistance to accept
What do you have to lose?
With everything to gain
Stop resisting the resistance
And live for the day
If you don't
You will continue to pay

Pay in ways that will continue to hurt
And stop you dead in your tracks
From ever gaining more then you have
Except two things
More pain and hurt
So, why can't you just accept?
That these issues are there
And just allow them to be there
Or are you too self-absorbed
Denying it
Rationalizing it
Justifying the resistance
Stop resisting the resistance
Can't you just accept it?
By allowing it to be there
If you don't stop the resistance to acceptance soon
It's going to stop you further
More than it has done now
Stop resisting the resistance
And accept it

Stubbornness and Willingness to Change

Why are you so stubborn?
Where is your willingness to change?
Why are you afraid to change?
I don't know how to change
I want to
But I'm afraid
It's the only way I've known
People didn't like me
People didn't want to understand me
So I would create ways to push them away
To keep them at bay
Or I'd find a way so I wouldn't have to stay
It's all I've known
To prevent the hurt
The hurt of rejection
Of a grander scale
I did at the start
In the hopes
People would see me for who I am
Beyond my perceived limitation
But now it's a part of me
A big part of me
But it's all I know
Can you give me the constructive guidance?
I need to change
I'm tired of being stubborn
And I'm willing to change
If you are willing to accept me
For the way I am right know
Until I learn a new way
But I'm also afraid

I'll turn you off
If you see the meek and mild me
For my stubbornness to change
Has given me the edge
The edge to survive
On my own
Alone
I want to stop using my stubborn excuses
As to why or why not
I have the willingness
When I see the way
To change my pattern
Yes, that stubborn pattern
That stands in the way
Of my becoming
The inspiration to myself
And of others
To accept the change
With willingness
The same willingness
That I am now stubborn to change
Only with the hope of a chance
And a change of attitudes
Of myself and others
With acceptance
Will the stubbornness go away willingly?
Help me find a better way

Take Everything I Have

Take everything I have
It does not mean a thing to me
For I have more in my heart and soul
Than I need of anything else
I'll even give you some of it
If you want or need it
For my purpose here is not to have needless things
But rather to share with you
From my heart
To teach and learn from you
If you want and are willing
Your truths are within you
As with everyone else
In doing so
I would be willing to give what it takes of my life
For you and others to benefit from my heart's knowledge
Within my heart's knowledge you can and will find some of your
    truths
If you're open to it and willing
To deny yourself this you will never know how we share and walk on
    other paths
You may say why should I know and walk on your path
Our paths are different but yet the same
For we seek the same things our own truths of our hearts and souls
    desire
I have been brought to you for a purpose
That purpose is to show you the same things I sought and found
The purity of heart and love that is not bound
Not bound in pain and disbelief of being real or unreal
A time of change is coming to you
If you let it
If you let me help to show it to you
Your choices to date have not helped you to propel yourself

To a most inspiring future
With and of purity of heart
Don't let your lack of acceptance of your positive heart's knowledge
    keep you stuck in the past
It does take discipline
And it may be painful while it is happening
But when you have sought, found and accepted the truths
Of your heart and soul's desire
You will have peace in your heart
And know the love you have
And the love you have to give
Take everything I have to give
Use it for your emotional gain
Use it to become more
So you have more to give
Learn from my knowledge
And share it with the ones you love
Or choose to love
But do not deny yourself that same love given
For then you have defeated the purpose of our meeting
Creator set forth this meeting
With an explicit purpose
That purpose was to show you
Show you that you are very worthy of new love
New love of yourself and another
Take everything I have
Every bit of knowledge
For it does not mean a thing to me
The only purpose for our meeting was for you to grow
From the knowledge of my heart and soul
For if I cannot pass on this knowledge Creator gave to me
I then have lost the purpose of our meeting
And I must move on more quickly than I thought
So I can share it with others needing this knowledge of love and life
That I was sent here to you to share
What I want for you does not matter
It is what you take from our meeting that counts

So take everything I have
It does not mean a thing to me
For I have more in my heart and soul to give
Than I need of anything else

"Look inside for the next best thing!
Be grateful for what you have,
for what is out there may not be what you need!"

Take the Easy Way Out

Hey, look! There's the back door
I'll just take the easy way out
No one will know
No one will care
But is it fair
That I take the easy way out
Just to maintain my health
So I don't have to work
But is maintaining my health my job?
Some days it seems so
Is it the easy way out?
Stretch this
Traction that
Lose that because you're too fat
Take this
Inject that
Lift this
Pull that
Eat this
Don't eat that
Drink this
Don't drink that
I think work is where it's at
It is a lot less work
I'll just take the easy way out
And go back to work

"Deal with the past,
Live in the present,
and have hope for the future!"

The Fix

Ah, the fix
The good old short term gratification
The release of brainless manifestations of needing (off)
To relieve the stress of your-pent up superficial life
Believing this is where life's at
The rush
Of short term gratification is only ripping you off
Don't you want to know?
Know about long term fulfilment
No, of course not
You'd have to change your behaviour
And deal with past pain
Oh, that fix
Where's the bottle
Where's the needle
Where's the smoke
Where's the food
Where's my booty
I need my fix
So you don't have to think
Take another drink
Man you're a dink
Looking for that fix so you don't have to think
That fix is only going to make you sink
Sink deeper into the depths of your own despair
That despair is truly unfair
May the buyer beware
Because the banker doesn't care
The banker isn't fair
You need your fix
To cover your tricks
For the need of that fix
Be careful now

That short term fix of gratification
May turn into more long term despair
That you think is unfair
And may be more then you can bear
When your debtors set up a snare
Because they don't care
Is that fix worth it?
Losing everything you have
Because that short term gratification
Just maybe it will turn into an addiction
Oh, that fix
Can play a trick
That can make you beyond sick
Just to cover up a need
A need for changing
How you deal with the issues in your life
Oh, that fix will take you
And everyone with you too
If you don't deal your issues through
That fix
Oh, that rush
It feels so good
And you don't want to give that up
But you know it's ripping you off
But it feels so good
What are you going to do?
Get stoned
Get laid
Get drunk
Or deal with the past issues that lead you here
To end the superficiality of your life
To become who your were intended to be
What are you going to do?
Time is ticking away
Are you going to stay?
In the here and now
Or are you going to seek the rush of another fix

So you can piss who and why you are away
It's your call
What are you going to do?
Just remember you have a reason to be here
Learn from your past
Remember nothing lasts
It is the past
But man, could it make your future a blast
So give yourself some sass
And deal with the past
In that you may find a new fix
Oh! With such a high
You'll feel like you're floating in the sky
Kissing the old fix goodbye
Because you found a better high
A better rush
And a new fix
Living and being who you were meant to be
Fixing the need for the fix
Will be the fix that set you free
Free to be high on your new breath of life
The life that you were meant to lead
Oh that fix
Oh that rush
That rush of life is meant to be your fix
So live the fix well
Being high on life's better
Don't you think?
Live your life to the fullest
Without the negative fix

"Follow your heart
For in that lies your destiny"

Good Morning, Mr. Pain

Good morning, Mr. Pain
I see you're still here
Lurking about, causing me despair
Will you ever leave me be?
You can take the corkscrew out of the base of my skull now
God, you exhaust me
It feels like I haven't slept a wink
Were you the cause of my bad dreams last night?
But then again you are a nightmare to me anyways
You woke me, I don't know how many times
With the pains, jerks, and spasms
Can't you just leave me alone for one night?
My fingers, hands and arms are numbed by you
And my arms feel like they been cut off with a hand saw
Man, I feel blah
You make Freddy Kroger look like a good boy
Instead of a killing toy
Sleep is supposed to be restful
Not this bleeding distressful
I got sharp pains in my neck, arms, and back
But again that's your knack
To give me all this flack
Why can't you cut me some slack?
My legs are like lead with numbness
Just like your dumbness
It feels like you're digging at my bone marrow

With some hideous tool of torture
Well, Mr. Pain, good morning
I guess you're here to stay
For the day
To keep my nerves a fray
So, I can have another sucky day

With you, Mr. Pain, there's no need to pray
Looks like you're never going to go away
Because you've settled in and are here to stay
Will I ever be able to say good bye to you, Mr. Pain
Or am I poised to live with you forever with distain
God, I know you're trying to drive me insane
Good morning, Mr. Pain
You are so unwelcome with distain

The Pain Is A Part Of Me

Do you know the concept of pain?
I'm sure you don't
You oh so normal judging person
I know the concept very well
You think I whine
It's in my head
Because you can't see it
With your eyes
You think I'm nuts
Maybe I am
But no more than you
You judge me
For what you can't see or feel
By all means I'll gladly give my pain to you
So you can conceptualize
What I go through and fear
I'll give you my pain
But only for a moment
Because I'm not mean
And I do not wish this pain onto anyone
But, I also know you will soon forget
What my pain feels like
And in time you'll judge me and my pain again
My pain is transient
It moves freely all over my body
I wish some days
I can be pain free
For but a moment
So I can think clearly
And freely walk around
Like you take for granted
Some days I cannot move
With or without tears and terrors of pain

The pain is driving me insane
So don't tell me you know the concept of pain
When clearly you don't
Do not pass judgement onto me
Because you can't see what's causing the pain
Just try to understand and accept
That some of my days are numbered
And I can't be or do
The things I once did
Just know I'll be there
When the pain is bearable
Love my good days
And tolerate the rest
The me you once knew is still here
It's being challenged by the pain
Understand my pain
Know I have it without question
When you can do that
You will see me to be true and real
Understanding you without judgement
For life's only sins
I now bear
Are the ones that lead me
To get me here
The pain you cannot see is real to me
So understand I'm in pain
Do not pass judgement onto me
For the pain is a part of me
But it is not me
It rips and tears at me
Like a cat in a cat fight
But the pain is not me
You think I can live
A normal life
Because you can't see the pain
I wish
I truly wish

Trust me, believe me, and accept me
For what I say
And who I am
My pain is real
It's never going to go away
However, my pain is not me
But is a part of me
If you cannot accept me
For the way I am
Please walk on
Because your unaccepting disbelief
Has become a pain to me
My pain is not me
It's a part of me

The Woman Wish List

The only way out is through
Let it go and let it flow
So here I go
Here's my women wish list
I hope no one will raise a fist
Because of my desired list
Someone may get pissed
Anyways, here's the dream list
Maybe someone will see the twist
Because it's just a fun list
We must be attractive to each other
But no other
She must be unwilling to smother
Me the other
She has to be smart
And be free to fart
Can be from any race
As long as she does not have a too-fast pace
She must be well adjusted
And not too heavily busted
She's mentally fit
And gives a shit
She must be healthy
But not mouthy
Must be a global thinker
And not a universal thought sinker
She must enjoy intimacy
With efficiency
Willing to settle down
But not downtown
She must have willingness to travel
Without going to unravel
Willingness to experiment with life

Without a knife
She must have dealt with abuse issues
And have no more need for tissues
She must be educated
Not infatuated
She must want or has children
But, does not have children of the corn
 She can be corny
And must be extremely horny
Must enjoy country life
Without strife
A willing to live in the East or have a cottage
So I don't have Ontario rottage
She must enjoy being doted over
Along with liking a good roll in the clover
Must be like minded but different
And not indifferent
Would be sufficient
She can deal with my health issues and pain
Without distain
Or leaving on the next train
She must be a life-long learner
And not a continuous pot burner
She must not smoke
I don't want her to look like old folk
Non materialistic
But realistic
Believes in me as a big part of the family
And not just around to be manly
She must believe in interconnectedness
And not co-dependantness
She must like to play
And want to stay
Stay till the ends of our day
And be willing to try and keep it that way
OK
She must be spiritual but not religiously bound

For I hate a bound new found
She must enjoy animals and nature
And not always the main feature
Because we're more healthy within nature
Which creates a better future
She must enjoy all seasons
Without a reason
She must enjoy camping
Whether or not she's cramping
My lady must be sexually adventurous
Without thinking it morally disastrous
She must enjoy a tidy house
So we're not chasing a mouse
And finally, she must enjoy us in good friendship
For it will always keep us pep
Remember I wrote this in fun
And not intended to make women run
But rather for us to have some fun
In the sun
Now I guess my list is done
So, will you stay or will you run

"I do not wish the desert of despair onto anyone
But I want to go into the desert from time to time
It is the only way one can be closer to themselves
To be with the pain that caused me sorrow
This torment and self questioning
Is the key that allows oneself to become closer to themselves
For it will allow me to become more humble and spiritual
So I can serve myself and others better"

Touch and Love

The feel
Of a touch
Of your skin
Your hair
Your heartbeat
Your sigh and a tear
In my hand is too valuable to lose!
We come in contact with oh so very few
That gives us this sense of wonderment
This pleasure
This sensation of love's destination
And determination
To survive
And be real in an oh so unreal world
Of what's in it for me, world
What happened to us?
And the grand sensation to share
And be with one
To share life's wonderment with
These simple joys of touch
And love's true becoming of itself
The feel of two souls touching
Is an explosive event
It is like the sun and snow becoming as one
To form a running brook that breathes new life
In the cool crisp spring air
What is life without touch?
And the sensation it gives?
For without it
Is there any quality of life?
And what of
Love's longing for itself?
Without touch

Are we bound not to know love's intent?
I hope not
For I cannot live without touch's sensation
And the bounty of the pleasure it gives
For I'd rather die than live without touch
And the wonderment of love brought to its knees through touch
For love cannot sustain itself without touch
Is there any truth to love without two souls touching?
Or is it just a mere facet of procreation
And sexual release
In a world gone mad to feed its greed
Of whatever that may be
Life may sustain itself
Through this madness
But what's the sense of going on
Without love and the touch of one another
I'd rather take death
Than not have love and touch
In my life
For love and touch have always had longing for each other
For they are the essence life itself
For the touching of two hearts is the beginning of life
And love's determination to survive

"You had my friendship from before we physically meet
As for being safe and loved that you are
I wouldn't have it any other way
For these things I commit to you"

Unlock Your Mind and We'll All Be Safe

The door behind you is now locked
And you think you're safe
Safe, from the outside world
But, are you safe? is the question
Because now you're alone
And you cannot lock the doors in your mind
What are your dangers you'll find?
Unlocked in your locked up mind
What have time and people done to you?
And you think you're safe behind your locked door
But really your dangers are your daily mental chore
And will have you bawling on the floor
You're not even safe behind a locked door
Because you can't lock your mind's door
Why are you reaching for that drug of choice?
To self-medicate from the dangers in your mind
Your own illegitimate tortures by design
Just so you can feel fine
For a time
Always blaming your issues on another's dime
When are you going to see the dangers are not out there?
But in your own mind
All the issues outside your locked door
Are the same dangers you face
When you unlock the mysteries of your mind
That you long since stashed away somewhere in your head
Dream on, if you think you're different
Different than the madness locked outside your door
You may snicker at the twisted fate of others and how they behave
Thinking you could never be as they
How do you know you're not already?

As you feed yourself with your own self indulgence
Indulgence to kill the pain of your own life disdain
The seeds of damage were put on you since birth
As with the ones outside your door
So are you really safe behind your locked door?
Or has the madness outside your door become an excuse?
So you don't have to look at your own issues of self-abuse
Caused by people and years gone bye
You're only safe for a while behind your door
Before you realize it's a chore
And you, sir, come to what has been done
And you can no longer hide
From your own dark side
And realize you have the same or similar issues as the others
And yes, there is a chance you are as them
But it's easy to say you're not
And deny yourself the truth
When sublimation of it can be done with self indulgence
But you cannot hide from the unlocked doors of your mind
Sooner or later the truth will be known
That their madness is your madness
And you'll have to do
What you indulged in not to?
And walk though all the painful doors
The doors that you shut over time
In order to say you're better than
You have your self control
The doors that say you're not like them
Doors that are nothing more then a mock-up of who you're not
Rather than doors that lead you to who you forgot
When you let go of your own falsehoods
And allow yourself to be
Be with who you are
And be with who you're meant to be
Without false need for a drug of choice
Then you have changed and set yourself free
Now

Just maybe you have good reason to be safe
Locking the door behind you

"I do not believe in strength in numbers
But, rather strength in our interconnectedness!"

Waiting to Secede

Oh, ye of little faith
We will return
Stronger and free
From our Canadian captors
Our once proud nation
We will raise the pink, white, and green once again
Some misty morn
Over our sacred shores of Newfoundland
And take our stand
As true Newfoundlanders
Free and strong
Oh, ye of little faith
We have stood for over five hundred years of admonitory
What's a few more
For our chance to succeed once again
We are of hearty stock
Willing to wait
For our time to secede from Canada
We are not indebted to Canada for our identity
We are true Newfoundlanders only indebted to ourselves
And the ones who died before us
We do not need the edicts of elsewhere to guide our path
But, rather follow our lead
We are Newfoundlanders
And are of the rock, wind and water
From which we etched out our existence
Before forced confederation with Canada
Oh ye of little faith
We shall remain
To take back our birthright
To raise the pink, white, and green
Over our proud nation, once again
We love thee Newfoundland

What Is Your Purpose?

We all have a purpose here
What is yours?
Or, do you prefer a self-defeated life
Marginalized by your own self doubt
Or your own self loathing
What is your purpose here?
Will you live up to your potential?
Or will you live for what others think you are?
Limiting you
By criticizing you
We've all been dealt our cards
And it's your move
What are you going to do?
Live the way others want and think of you
Or fill your purpose
And become who you were intended to be
Not just fantacizing about what could be
If you let it happen
It's your life
Live it
Fill your purpose and become more
And live the life you dreamt of
You can do it
Never mind the disbelieving doubters
They are not you
It does not matter about your circumstances right now
Start your change
Your steps need not be grand
But take your stand
Start living towards your purpose

It's your life
It's your dream
Live it
Live your purpose
With all the vigour you have in your dreams
So, what is your purpose here on earth?

What Keeps Me Tethered Here
(A Moment of Dark Thoughts)

What keeps me tethered to this world?
I have nothing really holding me
Other than my Mom and my niece
Yes, there are friends
Some dearer than others
There is an ex-wife and ex-girlfriends
But do they count?
I have brothers and sisters and other relatives
But they don't matter
So, what keeps me tethered to this world?
Am I holding onto something make-believe?
This thing called life
Is there anything that is to become of me?
Taking away all I have and all I'm going to have
Is nothing to me
I have nothing worth taking or having
So what tethers me to this world?
I have chronic pain
Sleep disorders
And the list goes on
I'm doing all I can do to deal with it
Am I going to be forced back to work
So I can't maintain my health, as easily
Why not cut the tether and leave this world?
My love life sucks
Gee, is it because of my health?
And I have no financial security
So what keeps me tethered to this earth?
All I have to offer is myself
And gifts of knowledge I may have
I have the equipment

And I don't need a manual to use it
But that's not what they want
So, why stay tethered to this place called the land of the living?
I have no reason to stay
Or do I
Could it be my gifts of knowledge that the wayward of heart seek?
My little knowledge of the heart, love and life
Are these the reasons I should keep tethered to this pitiful place called
    earth?
But why offer up this knowledge?
When I am denied by God the very thing they seek
I am not a Prophet
For the pain of being alone is just as painful
As the physical pain
I am forced to suffer
From the hands of myself and my God
So why should I stay tethered here on earth?
People question my health
Because I, for the most part, hide my pain with a happy face
They don't know what I go through
Silently
Some call me a faker
Some call me a cheat
I wish they could see and feel what I go through
On a bad day
But, they can't or won't see
So why, oh bloody why should I stay tethered here?
On this hell called earth
If I can't live a life
With love and dignity
Without always fighting for it
Without change to what they want me to be
May my tethering to this earth be severed swiftly
For I am tired
Oh, so very tired
And I am finding it too hard to fight
Fight for my right to live

All men die
Very few will ever truly live
So why should I stay tethered here?
What's left to give?
God take me home, any time soon

"Enjoy the ride life gives you
But sometimes consider sharing it with a friend
Because getting to your destination can be so much more fun
And it could lead to a whole new journey in the end"

What of Beauty?

What of beauty?
Beauty is life's thirsting for itself
For beauty is not just a living thing
But a feeling that touches your soul
And leaves you in awe
Beauty is the rising of the morning sun
And the sun going down at night
Beauty is the moon and stars on a clear night
Beauty is in all living things
As beauty lies in non-living things as well
Beauty lies in the souls of all men
Once you shed the pain of life's experience
And the true soul be seen
As with all of man, beauty as seen in their eyes can be misunderstood
    and disliked
This misunderstanding and dislike comes from the reflection you see
    looking back at you
Yet this misunderstanding and dislike is beauty in disguise
Waiting for you to work on and love your beauty within
When your true self be seen beauty will be abound
But yet, I know this is not the question of beauty you seek
You seek the superficial aspects of beauty
For this I cannot answer
Beauty is in everything I feel and see
As for the sexes, beauty lies in the essence of their being
And not how they look or act
Beauty is their soul's depth
Their passion and convictions
Their spiritual connectedness and the aura they carry
Beauty is the gentleness of their being
As if their life is set out by angels
Beauty is the true connectedness of the souls' meeting
It is like the rising of the morning sun

The evening sunset at day's end
And the rising of the moon and the stars at night
To light your way
With that beauty is forever more
For beauty is life itself
As set out by the Gods
For you to see
That beauty abounds
And waits for you to truly see beauty for what it is
For it is everything that life holds for you and more
You just have to open your mind
Open your heart
And listen
Listen to your innermost being
Listen to your soul
For beauty is in everything
And beauty only has longing for you to see
That it starts by acceptance of the one
Looking back in the looking glass
And that is the start of all beautiful things

"Find yourself love
and true love will find you again!"

Vision Statement

I will become more spiritual and humble though my continued commitment and development of myself. So I can accept, love, and understand myself, my Creator and others better!

You are a Masterpiece onto Yourself

You are a master piece onto yourself
Why apply more falsehoods?
For depths of deceit
And colour unbecoming
Your masterpiece came from the bushes of the gods that created you
Why do you feel you have to distort it?
With things that you need not be bothered with
Hiding behind pounds of pain and shame
Why must you play with the artisan's brush like that?
The only thing you should do to a masterpiece like yourself
Is to clean the stains of time off, now and again
Your beauty does not need a total overhaul
Crud does build up over time
But can be easily managed
If you're willing to do the work
Of dealing with the hurt
We bear onto ourselves from time to time
Oh yes, we do tend to blame others for that hurt
But ultimately, it is we who allow it to damage our masterpiece
By accepting it as a part of our picture
And allowing ourselves to brush these falsehoods on
Distorting the masterpiece of who we are
You are a masterpiece onto yourself
In order to show and reveal the true nature of this masterpiece
You are going to have to do a deep cleaning
By scraping off the deep layers of self deceit, falsehoods
And colour unbecoming
To show the true beauty and nature of you, the master piece
Followed by touch-ups from time to time
To keep the masterpiece glistening throughout time
Because you are a masterpiece onto yourself

You Passed Judgement on Me Today

You passed judgement on me today
Why?
Or was it a projection
You said I don't love myself
What makes you think that?
Why do you think that?
Very frankly, I don't care
I love you either way
You said I don't love myself
Because I said I don't care if I live or die
To me my life has no real meaning
Without responsibility, want and need to be wanted in my life
Yes, I have lived a life
One not exactly as I wanted
But I have lived a life
It does not mean I don't love myself
It does not mean I don't love my life
But what is life
Without a love of another
To share it with
What is life without direction or real purpose?
What is life with pain?
And others saying
Get over it
Quit the whining
Stop the pity party
Oh poor you
You passed judgement on me today
Because you perceived
I don't love myself
Because I said I don't care if I live or die

I love myself more than you know
Because if I didn't love myself
How can I honestly say
'I love you' to another and mean it?
What are you afraid of?
You passed judgement on me today
Without knowing I'm real, here and in the now
Loving you unconditionally
Without passing judgement on you
Just loving you for you
Knowing I can because I love myself
Accepting your reasons
Of why, or why not, you can or cannot
So, why must you pass judgement on me?
Can't you just love me for me?
If you cannot love me for me
Is it because you're still searching
For yourself to love
You are my friend
I love you very much
Just accept me for me
And love me just the way I am
Please don't pass judgement on me
Today or any day
That is God's job and God's job alone to do

"May you wake in the morn
Like the sunshine across the horizon!"

You're Only Jailed by Your Past

If you don't face the past
You'll stay stuck in it
And never see the future
Or have a future in the here and now
But one of dreams of could a should a
Maybe if I
Deal with the past
You'll live in the present
And have a future worth looking forward to
Not dealing with the past the rewards are few
You're held by demons past
Demons that should have been dealt with
For they are jailing you
Jailing you inside yourself
Tormenting you endlessly
Keeping you from being more
Holding you back
From a future worth living
One of the here and now
One with no pain of past sins
But rather one of joy and riches
Gained by them
Riches of love friendship and belonging
Stop longing for more
Deal with the past
Be content with who you are
And what you have
In the here and now
The pain of past sins
Is keeping you from achieving
Achieving your future goals
Stop the jailer from jailing you further
Deal with the past

To have the future you always wanted
One with love respect and achievement
The same one you longed for
When you let undealt past sins jail you
Have faith in yourself
That things can change
And improve for the better
If only you accept past sins
And not use them as excuses
Excuses that keep you held
Held to past behaviours
Deal with them and let them go
Only then past sins against you
Will no longer imprison you
From your full potential
And having the future you dreamt of
And deserve
The one with love, honour, respect, and achievement
So stop the jailer from jailing you
And Live
Live
Live your life to the fullest
The way you dreamt of

"No matter where or how long our journey together takes us
Just know you're loved by me unconditionally"

Thank you for reading my work, I hope you enjoyed it!
Keith

About the author

Keith Power grew up in Cumberland County, Nova Scotia and spent most of his adult life in Hastings County Ontario. He presently resides north of Kingston, Ontario.

Keith Power has worked in the Human Services and Educational sector for over twenty years.

Due to personal loss and physical illness Keith, through writing and soap stone carving, found a mindful way of dealing with his pain. Living with a Madman in Tow and his Spirit Guide carving are his first works and have helped him find a new focus away from the pain and towards something more hopeful.

LaVergne, TN USA
28 October 2009
162215LV00001B/52/P